50 Vegan Barbecue Recipes for Home

By: Kelly Johnson

Table of Contents

- Grilled Portobello Mushroom Burgers
- Barbecue Jackfruit Sandwiches
- Vegan BBQ Tempeh Skewers
- Grilled Vegetable Kebabs with BBQ Sauce
- Vegan BBQ Tofu Steaks
- BBQ Cauliflower Wings
- Vegan BBQ Chickpea Burgers
- Grilled Corn on the Cob with BBQ Seasoning
- BBQ Seitan Ribs
- Grilled Pineapple Slices with BBQ Glaze
- BBQ Lentil Sloppy Joes
- Vegan BBQ Potato Salad
- BBQ Tempeh Bacon
- Grilled Zucchini with BBQ Rub
- Vegan BBQ Pulled Mushroom Sandwiches
- BBQ Portobello Mushroom Steaks
- Grilled Tofu Skewers with BBQ Marinade
- Vegan BBQ Meatballs
- BBQ Chickpea Stuffed Bell Peppers
- Grilled Eggplant with BBQ Sauce
- Vegan BBQ Cauliflower Steaks
- BBQ Black Bean Burgers
- Grilled Asparagus with BBQ Seasoning
- BBQ Seitan Skewers with Vegetables
- Vegan BBQ Jackfruit Tacos
- BBQ Sweet Potato Wedges
- Grilled Avocado with BBQ Drizzle
- Vegan BBQ Beans
- BBQ Tempeh Sliders
- Grilled Portobello Mushroom Fajitas with BBQ Sauce
- BBQ Tofu Nuggets
- Vegan BBQ Stuffed Bell Peppers
- Grilled Pineapple and Avocado Salad with BBQ Dressing
- BBQ Cauliflower Tacos
- Vegan BBQ Slaw

- Grilled Watermelon with BBQ Rub
- BBQ Seitan Sandwiches
- Vegan BBQ Stuffed Potatoes
- Grilled Sweet Potato and Black Bean Salad with BBQ Dressing
- BBQ Tempeh Tacos
- Vegan BBQ Jackfruit Pizza
- Grilled Corn and Black Bean Salad with BBQ Dressing
- BBQ Chickpea Wraps
- Grilled Romaine Lettuce with BBQ Drizzle
- BBQ Portobello Mushroom Tacos
- Vegan BBQ Pasta Salad
- Grilled Veggie Quesadillas with BBQ Sauce
- BBQ Tofu Stir Fry
- Vegan BBQ Nachos
- Grilled Peach Slices with BBQ Glaze

Grilled Portobello Mushroom Burgers

Ingredients:

- 4 large portobello mushrooms, stems removed
- 1/4 cup balsamic vinegar
- 2 tablespoons olive oil
- 2 cloves garlic, minced
- 1 teaspoon dried thyme
- Salt and pepper to taste
- 4 burger buns
- Optional toppings: lettuce, tomato, avocado, vegan cheese, vegan mayonnaise, etc.

Instructions:

In a shallow dish, whisk together balsamic vinegar, olive oil, minced garlic, dried thyme, salt, and pepper to create a marinade.
Place the portobello mushrooms in the marinade, turning to coat each side. Let them marinate for at least 20-30 minutes, flipping halfway through if possible.
Preheat your grill to medium-high heat.
Remove the mushrooms from the marinade and shake off any excess. Reserve the marinade for basting.
Place the mushrooms on the preheated grill, gill side down. Grill for about 4-5 minutes on each side, or until they are tender and have grill marks.
While the mushrooms are grilling, you can toast the burger buns on the grill if desired.
Brush the reserved marinade onto the mushrooms occasionally while grilling to add flavor.
Once the mushrooms are cooked through, remove them from the grill and assemble your burgers with your desired toppings on the toasted buns.
Serve immediately and enjoy your delicious Grilled Portobello Mushroom Burgers!

Feel free to customize your burgers with your favorite toppings and condiments to suit your taste preferences. Enjoy!

Barbecue Jackfruit Sandwiches

Ingredients:

- 2 cans young green jackfruit in water or brine, drained and rinsed
- 1 tablespoon olive oil
- 1/2 onion, finely chopped
- 2 cloves garlic, minced
- 1 cup barbecue sauce (use your favorite vegan variety)
- 1/4 cup vegetable broth or water
- Salt and pepper to taste
- 4 hamburger buns
- Optional toppings: coleslaw, pickles, vegan cheese, sliced onions, etc.

Instructions:

Heat olive oil in a large skillet over medium heat. Add the chopped onion and garlic, and sauté until softened, about 3-4 minutes.
Add the drained and rinsed jackfruit to the skillet. Use a fork or potato masher to break up the jackfruit into smaller pieces, resembling shredded meat.
Cook the jackfruit for 5-7 minutes, stirring occasionally, until it begins to brown slightly.
Pour in the barbecue sauce and vegetable broth or water, stirring to combine.
Reduce the heat to low and simmer for 15-20 minutes, stirring occasionally, until the jackfruit is tender and the sauce has thickened.
Use a fork to further shred the jackfruit if desired, to achieve a more pulled texture.
Season with salt and pepper to taste, and adjust the barbecue sauce if needed.
While the jackfruit is simmering, you can toast the hamburger buns if desired.
Once the jackfruit is done cooking, assemble your sandwiches by spooning the barbecue jackfruit onto the bottom halves of the hamburger buns.
Add your desired toppings, such as coleslaw, pickles, vegan cheese, sliced onions, etc.
Place the top halves of the hamburger buns over the filling to complete the sandwiches.
Serve hot and enjoy your delicious Barbecue Jackfruit Sandwiches!

These sandwiches are packed with flavor and make for a satisfying vegan barbecue meal. Feel free to adjust the seasonings and toppings to suit your taste preferences. Enjoy!

Vegan BBQ Tempeh Skewers

Ingredients:

- 8 oz (225g) tempeh, cut into cubes
- 1 red bell pepper, cut into chunks
- 1 green bell pepper, cut into chunks
- 1 red onion, cut into chunks
- 8-10 cherry tomatoes
- For the BBQ Marinade:
    - 1/4 cup barbecue sauce (ensure it's vegan)
    - 2 tablespoons soy sauce or tamari
    - 2 tablespoons maple syrup or agave nectar
    - 1 tablespoon olive oil
    - 2 cloves garlic, minced
    - 1 teaspoon smoked paprika
    - Salt and pepper to taste
- Wooden or metal skewers, if using wooden skewers, soak them in water for 30 minutes before using to prevent burning

Instructions:

In a small bowl, whisk together all the ingredients for the BBQ marinade until well combined.

Place the cubed tempeh, bell pepper chunks, onion chunks, and cherry tomatoes in a large bowl or shallow dish. Pour the marinade over the tempeh and vegetables, making sure everything is evenly coated. Marinate for at least 30 minutes, or overnight for stronger flavor.

Preheat your grill to medium-high heat.

Thread the marinated tempeh, bell peppers, onions, and cherry tomatoes onto the skewers, alternating the ingredients as desired.

Once the grill is hot, lightly oil the grill grates to prevent sticking. Place the skewers on the grill and cook for 10-12 minutes, turning occasionally, until the tempeh and vegetables are lightly charred and cooked through.

While grilling, you can brush some extra marinade onto the skewers for added flavor.

Once cooked, remove the skewers from the grill and transfer them to a serving platter.

Serve the Vegan BBQ Tempeh Skewers hot, garnished with chopped fresh herbs if desired.

Enjoy your delicious barbecue tempeh skewers as a main dish or alongside your favorite side dishes.

These skewers are packed with flavor and make for a hearty and satisfying vegan barbecue meal. Feel free to customize the vegetables and adjust the seasonings to suit your taste preferences. Enjoy!

Grilled Vegetable Kebabs with BBQ Sauce

Ingredients:

- 2 bell peppers (any color), cut into chunks
- 1 zucchini, sliced into rounds
- 1 yellow squash, sliced into rounds
- 1 red onion, cut into chunks
- 8-10 cherry tomatoes
- For the BBQ Sauce:
    - 1/2 cup barbecue sauce (ensure it's vegan)
    - 2 tablespoons olive oil
    - 2 tablespoons soy sauce or tamari
    - 1 tablespoon maple syrup or agave nectar
    - 2 cloves garlic, minced
    - 1 teaspoon smoked paprika
    - Salt and pepper to taste
- Wooden or metal skewers, if using wooden skewers, soak them in water for 30 minutes before using to prevent burning

Instructions:

In a small bowl, whisk together all the ingredients for the BBQ sauce until well combined.

Place the bell pepper chunks, zucchini slices, yellow squash slices, red onion chunks, and cherry tomatoes in a large bowl or shallow dish. Pour half of the BBQ sauce over the vegetables, reserving the other half for basting while grilling. Toss to coat the vegetables evenly. Marinate for at least 30 minutes, or longer for stronger flavor.

Preheat your grill to medium-high heat.

Thread the marinated vegetables onto the skewers, alternating the vegetables as desired.

Once the grill is hot, lightly oil the grill grates to prevent sticking. Place the vegetable kebabs on the grill and cook for 10-12 minutes, turning occasionally, until the vegetables are tender and lightly charred.

While grilling, brush the remaining BBQ sauce onto the kebabs for added flavor. Once cooked, remove the vegetable kebabs from the grill and transfer them to a serving platter.

Serve the Grilled Vegetable Kebabs with BBQ Sauce hot, garnished with chopped fresh herbs if desired.

Enjoy your delicious barbecue vegetable kebabs as a main dish or alongside your favorite side dishes.

These kebabs are not only colorful and flavorful but also packed with nutrients, making them a perfect addition to any vegan barbecue spread. Feel free to customize the vegetables and adjust the seasonings to suit your taste preferences. Enjoy!

Vegan BBQ Tofu Steaks

Ingredients:

- 1 block (14-16 oz) extra-firm tofu, pressed and drained
- 1/4 cup barbecue sauce (ensure it's vegan)
- 2 tablespoons soy sauce or tamari
- 1 tablespoon maple syrup or agave nectar
- 1 tablespoon olive oil
- 2 cloves garlic, minced
- 1 teaspoon smoked paprika
- Salt and pepper to taste

Instructions:

Preheat your oven to 375°F (190°C).
In a small bowl, whisk together the barbecue sauce, soy sauce or tamari, maple syrup or agave nectar, olive oil, minced garlic, smoked paprika, salt, and pepper to make the marinade.
Cut the pressed and drained tofu block into 4 equal-sized steaks.
Place the tofu steaks in a shallow dish or a large resealable plastic bag. Pour the marinade over the tofu steaks, making sure they are evenly coated. Marinate for at least 30 minutes, or longer for stronger flavor, flipping the steaks halfway through if using a dish.
Heat a non-stick skillet over medium-high heat. Once hot, add the marinated tofu steaks to the skillet, reserving the marinade.
Cook the tofu steaks for 3-4 minutes on each side, or until lightly browned and caramelized.
While the tofu is cooking, transfer the reserved marinade to a small saucepan. Bring it to a simmer over medium heat and cook for 2-3 minutes, stirring occasionally, until slightly thickened. This will be used as a glaze for the tofu steaks.
Transfer the partially cooked tofu steaks to a baking dish lined with parchment paper or lightly greased. Brush the tofu steaks with the thickened marinade, coating them evenly.
Bake the tofu steaks in the preheated oven for 15-20 minutes, or until they are firm and have absorbed the flavors.

Once cooked, remove the tofu steaks from the oven and let them cool for a few minutes before serving.

Serve the Vegan BBQ Tofu Steaks hot, garnished with chopped fresh herbs if desired.

Enjoy your delicious barbecue tofu steaks as a main dish or alongside your favorite side dishes.

These tofu steaks are packed with flavor and have a satisfyingly chewy texture, making them a perfect centerpiece for any vegan barbecue meal. Feel free to customize the marinade and adjust the seasonings to suit your taste preferences. Enjoy!

BBQ Cauliflower Wings

Ingredients:

- 1 head cauliflower, cut into florets
- 3/4 cup all-purpose flour (or chickpea flour for gluten-free option)
- 3/4 cup unsweetened plant-based milk (such as almond milk or soy milk)
- 1 teaspoon garlic powder
- 1 teaspoon onion powder
- 1/2 teaspoon smoked paprika
- Salt and pepper to taste
- 1 cup barbecue sauce (ensure it's vegan)
- 2 tablespoons melted vegan butter or olive oil
- Optional: chopped fresh parsley or cilantro for garnish

Instructions:

Preheat your oven to 450°F (230°C). Line a baking sheet with parchment paper or lightly grease it.

In a mixing bowl, whisk together the flour, plant-based milk, garlic powder, onion powder, smoked paprika, salt, and pepper until you have a smooth batter.

Dip each cauliflower floret into the batter, making sure it's evenly coated, and shake off any excess batter.

Place the battered cauliflower florets on the prepared baking sheet in a single layer, leaving space between each floret.

Bake the cauliflower in the preheated oven for 20-25 minutes, or until they are golden brown and crispy, flipping them halfway through.

While the cauliflower is baking, in a small saucepan, combine the barbecue sauce and melted vegan butter or olive oil. Heat the sauce over low heat, stirring occasionally, until warmed through.

Once the cauliflower wings are done baking, remove them from the oven and transfer them to a large mixing bowl.

Pour the warm barbecue sauce mixture over the cauliflower wings and toss until they are evenly coated.

Return the coated cauliflower wings to the baking sheet and bake for an additional 5-10 minutes, or until the sauce is caramelized and sticky.

Remove the cauliflower wings from the oven and let them cool for a few minutes before serving.

Garnish with chopped fresh parsley or cilantro if desired.
Serve the BBQ Cauliflower Wings hot with your favorite dipping sauce, such as vegan ranch or vegan blue cheese dressing.
Enjoy your delicious barbecue cauliflower wings as a tasty appetizer or snack!

These BBQ cauliflower wings are crispy on the outside, tender on the inside, and bursting with flavor. They're perfect for serving at parties, game nights, or as a fun appetizer for any occasion. Feel free to adjust the seasonings and sauce to suit your taste preferences. Enjoy!

Vegan BBQ Chickpea Burgers

Ingredients:

- 2 cans (15 ounces each) chickpeas, drained and rinsed
- 1/2 cup bread crumbs (use gluten-free if needed)
- 1/4 cup finely chopped red onion
- 1/4 cup finely chopped bell pepper (any color)
- 2 cloves garlic, minced
- 2 tablespoons barbecue sauce (ensure it's vegan)
- 1 tablespoon soy sauce or tamari
- 1 tablespoon ground flaxseed meal + 3 tablespoons water (or use a flax egg)
- 1 teaspoon smoked paprika
- 1/2 teaspoon ground cumin
- Salt and pepper to taste
- Olive oil or cooking spray for frying
- Burger buns and toppings of choice (lettuce, tomato, avocado, vegan cheese, etc.)

Instructions:

In a small bowl, mix together the ground flaxseed meal and water. Let it sit for 5-10 minutes to thicken and form a flax egg.
In a large mixing bowl, mash the chickpeas with a fork or potato masher until they are mostly broken down but still have some texture.
Add the bread crumbs, chopped red onion, chopped bell pepper, minced garlic, barbecue sauce, soy sauce or tamari, smoked paprika, ground cumin, salt, pepper, and prepared flax egg to the mashed chickpeas. Mix until well combined.
Divide the mixture into 4 equal portions and shape each portion into a burger patty.
Heat a skillet over medium heat and lightly coat it with olive oil or cooking spray. Place the chickpea burger patties in the skillet and cook for 4-5 minutes on each side, or until golden brown and heated through.
While the burgers are cooking, toast the burger buns if desired.
Once the chickpea burgers are cooked, assemble them on the burger buns with your favorite toppings, such as lettuce, tomato, avocado, vegan cheese, etc.
Serve the Vegan BBQ Chickpea Burgers hot and enjoy!

These chickpea burgers are flavorful, hearty, and perfect for a vegan barbecue or a quick weeknight meal. Feel free to customize the seasonings and toppings to suit your taste preferences. Enjoy!

Grilled Corn on the Cob with BBQ Seasoning

Ingredients:

- 4 ears of corn, husks removed
- 2 tablespoons olive oil
- BBQ seasoning mix (you can use store-bought or make your own with a combination of paprika, garlic powder, onion powder, smoked paprika, cumin, chili powder, salt, and pepper)
- Optional: vegan butter or margarine for serving

Instructions:

Preheat your grill to medium-high heat.
Brush each ear of corn with olive oil, ensuring they are evenly coated.
Sprinkle BBQ seasoning mix over the oiled corn, rolling them to ensure all sides are covered with the seasoning.
Place the seasoned corn directly on the grill grates.
Grill the corn for about 10-12 minutes, turning occasionally, until the kernels are tender and lightly charred.
Once the corn is cooked, remove it from the grill and transfer it to a serving platter.
Optionally, top each ear of corn with a pat of vegan butter or margarine while still hot.
Serve the grilled corn on the cob with BBQ seasoning immediately.
Enjoy your delicious and flavorful barbecue-style corn on the cob!

This dish is perfect for summer cookouts, barbecues, or as a side dish for any meal. The smoky flavors from the BBQ seasoning combined with the sweetness of the corn make for a winning combination. Feel free to adjust the seasoning according to your taste preferences. Enjoy!

BBQ Seitan Ribs

Ingredients:

For the Seitan Ribs:

- 2 cups vital wheat gluten
- 1/4 cup nutritional yeast
- 2 teaspoons onion powder
- 2 teaspoons garlic powder
- 1 teaspoon smoked paprika
- 1 teaspoon dried thyme
- 1 teaspoon dried oregano
- 1 cup vegetable broth
- 2 tablespoons soy sauce or tamari
- 2 tablespoons tomato paste
- 1 tablespoon olive oil
- 1 tablespoon vegan Worcestershire sauce
- 1 tablespoon liquid smoke
- Salt and pepper to taste

For the BBQ Sauce:

- 1 cup barbecue sauce (ensure it's vegan)
- 2 tablespoons apple cider vinegar
- 1 tablespoon maple syrup or agave nectar
- 1 tablespoon Dijon mustard
- 1 teaspoon smoked paprika
- 1/2 teaspoon garlic powder
- Salt and pepper to taste

Instructions:

Preheat your oven to 350°F (175°C). Lightly grease a baking dish or line it with parchment paper.
In a large mixing bowl, combine the vital wheat gluten, nutritional yeast, onion powder, garlic powder, smoked paprika, dried thyme, and dried oregano.

In a separate bowl, whisk together the vegetable broth, soy sauce or tamari, tomato paste, olive oil, vegan Worcestershire sauce, and liquid smoke.

Pour the wet ingredients into the dry ingredients and mix until a dough forms.

Knead the dough for a few minutes to develop the gluten.

Shape the dough into a rectangle slab resembling ribs.

Place the seitan rib slab in the prepared baking dish.

In a small bowl, mix together all the ingredients for the BBQ sauce until well combined.

Pour half of the BBQ sauce over the seitan rib slab, spreading it evenly to coat.

Cover the baking dish with aluminum foil and bake in the preheated oven for 30 minutes.

Remove the foil and carefully flip the seitan rib slab. Pour the remaining BBQ sauce over the top, spreading it evenly.

Bake, uncovered, for an additional 15-20 minutes, or until the seitan ribs are firm and golden brown.

Once cooked, remove the seitan ribs from the oven and let them cool for a few minutes before slicing and serving.

Serve the BBQ Seitan Ribs hot, garnished with chopped fresh herbs if desired.

Enjoy your delicious barbecue-style seitan ribs as a main dish or alongside your favorite side dishes!

These seitan ribs are tender, chewy, and packed with flavor, making them a perfect vegan alternative for barbecue enthusiasts. Adjust the seasoning and barbecue sauce according to your taste preferences. Enjoy!

Grilled Pineapple Slices with BBQ Glaze

Ingredients:

- 1 large pineapple, peeled, cored, and sliced into rings
- 1/2 cup barbecue sauce (ensure it's vegan)
- 2 tablespoons maple syrup or agave nectar
- 1 tablespoon soy sauce or tamari
- 1 teaspoon smoked paprika
- 1/2 teaspoon garlic powder
- Olive oil or cooking spray for greasing the grill

Instructions:

Preheat your grill to medium-high heat.
In a small bowl, whisk together the barbecue sauce, maple syrup or agave nectar, soy sauce or tamari, smoked paprika, and garlic powder until well combined. This is your BBQ glaze.
Lightly grease the grill grates with olive oil or cooking spray to prevent sticking.
Place the pineapple slices directly onto the preheated grill.
Grill the pineapple slices for about 3-4 minutes on each side, or until they have grill marks and are slightly caramelized.
Once the pineapple slices are grilled on both sides, brush them generously with the BBQ glaze, coating each slice evenly.
Continue grilling the pineapple slices for an additional 1-2 minutes on each side, brushing them with more BBQ glaze as needed, until the glaze is caramelized and sticky.
Once cooked, remove the grilled pineapple slices from the grill and transfer them to a serving platter.
Optionally, garnish the grilled pineapple slices with chopped fresh herbs like mint or cilantro for extra flavor and presentation.
Serve the Grilled Pineapple Slices with BBQ Glaze hot or at room temperature as a delicious side dish or dessert.
Enjoy the sweet and tangy flavors of these grilled pineapple slices with BBQ glaze!

These grilled pineapple slices are perfect for summer barbecues, picnics, or as a refreshing dessert. The combination of smoky, sweet, and tangy flavors will tantalize your taste buds. Feel free to adjust the seasoning and sweetness of the BBQ glaze according to your preferences. Enjoy!

BBQ Lentil Sloppy Joes

Ingredients:

- 1 cup dry lentils, rinsed and drained
- 3 cups vegetable broth
- 1 tablespoon olive oil
- 1 onion, finely chopped
- 2 cloves garlic, minced
- 1 bell pepper, diced
- 1 cup tomato sauce
- 1/4 cup barbecue sauce (ensure it's vegan)
- 1 tablespoon maple syrup or brown sugar
- 1 tablespoon soy sauce or tamari
- 1 teaspoon smoked paprika
- 1/2 teaspoon chili powder
- Salt and pepper to taste
- Hamburger buns, for serving
- Optional toppings: sliced avocado, vegan cheese, sliced pickles, coleslaw, etc.

Instructions:

In a medium saucepan, combine the lentils and vegetable broth. Bring to a boil, then reduce the heat to low, cover, and simmer for 20-25 minutes, or until the lentils are tender and the liquid is absorbed. Drain any excess liquid and set aside.
In a large skillet, heat the olive oil over medium heat. Add the chopped onion and bell pepper, and cook for 5-7 minutes, or until softened.
Add the minced garlic to the skillet and cook for an additional 1-2 minutes, until fragrant.
Stir in the cooked lentils, tomato sauce, barbecue sauce, maple syrup or brown sugar, soy sauce or tamari, smoked paprika, chili powder, salt, and pepper. Mix well to combine.
Reduce the heat to low and simmer the mixture for 10-15 minutes, stirring occasionally, until the flavors are well blended and the mixture has thickened.
While the mixture is simmering, toast the hamburger buns if desired.
Once the lentil sloppy joe mixture is ready, spoon it onto the bottom halves of the hamburger buns.

Top with your favorite toppings, such as sliced avocado, vegan cheese, sliced pickles, coleslaw, etc.
Place the top halves of the hamburger buns over the filling to complete the sandwiches.
Serve the BBQ Lentil Sloppy Joes hot and enjoy!

These BBQ lentil sloppy joes are hearty, flavorful, and perfect for a vegan barbecue or weeknight dinner. Feel free to customize the seasoning and toppings to suit your taste preferences. Enjoy!

Vegan BBQ Potato Salad

Ingredients:

- 2 lbs (about 1 kg) potatoes, peeled and cubed
- 1/2 cup vegan mayonnaise
- 2 tablespoons barbecue sauce (ensure it's vegan)
- 1 tablespoon Dijon mustard
- 1 tablespoon apple cider vinegar
- 1/4 cup finely chopped red onion
- 1/4 cup finely chopped celery
- 2 tablespoons finely chopped fresh parsley
- Salt and pepper to taste
- Optional: sliced green onions for garnish

Instructions:

Place the cubed potatoes in a large pot and cover with water. Add a pinch of salt to the water.

Bring the water to a boil over medium-high heat, then reduce the heat to medium-low and simmer for 10-15 minutes, or until the potatoes are fork-tender.

Drain the cooked potatoes and transfer them to a large mixing bowl. Let them cool for a few minutes.

In a small bowl, whisk together the vegan mayonnaise, barbecue sauce, Dijon mustard, and apple cider vinegar until well combined.

Pour the dressing over the cooked potatoes in the mixing bowl. Gently toss until the potatoes are evenly coated with the dressing.

Add the finely chopped red onion, celery, and fresh parsley to the bowl with the dressed potatoes. Stir to combine.

Season the potato salad with salt and pepper to taste. Adjust the seasoning as needed.

Cover the potato salad and refrigerate for at least 1 hour before serving to allow the flavors to meld together.

Before serving, give the potato salad a final stir and taste test, adjusting the seasoning if necessary.

Garnish the potato salad with sliced green onions, if desired.

Serve the Vegan BBQ Potato Salad chilled or at room temperature as a delicious side dish for your barbecue or picnic.

This vegan BBQ potato salad is creamy, tangy, and packed with flavor, making it the perfect accompaniment to grilled dishes or as a standalone dish for gatherings. Enjoy!

BBQ Tempeh Bacon

Ingredients:

- 1 block (8 oz) tempeh
- 2 tablespoons soy sauce or tamari
- 1 tablespoon maple syrup
- 1 tablespoon olive oil
- 1 tablespoon tomato paste
- 1 teaspoon liquid smoke
- 1 teaspoon smoked paprika
- 1/2 teaspoon garlic powder
- 1/2 teaspoon onion powder
- 1/4 teaspoon black pepper
- 1/4 teaspoon cayenne pepper (optional, for heat)
- 2 tablespoons barbecue sauce (ensure it's vegan)

Instructions:

Slice the tempeh into thin strips, about 1/8 to 1/4 inch thick. You can slice it lengthwise or widthwise, depending on your preference.
In a shallow dish or bowl, whisk together the soy sauce or tamari, maple syrup, olive oil, tomato paste, liquid smoke, smoked paprika, garlic powder, onion powder, black pepper, and cayenne pepper (if using) to make the marinade.
Place the tempeh strips in the marinade, ensuring they are evenly coated. Let them marinate for at least 30 minutes, or longer for more flavor, flipping them halfway through if possible.
Preheat your oven to 375°F (190°C). Line a baking sheet with parchment paper or lightly grease it.
Arrange the marinated tempeh strips on the prepared baking sheet in a single layer, leaving space between each strip.
Bake the tempeh in the preheated oven for 15-20 minutes, flipping halfway through, or until the edges are crispy and golden brown.
Remove the tempeh from the oven and brush each strip with barbecue sauce. Return the tempeh to the oven and bake for an additional 5-10 minutes, or until the barbecue sauce is caramelized and sticky.
Once cooked, remove the BBQ tempeh bacon from the oven and let it cool for a few minutes before serving.

Serve the BBQ Tempeh Bacon as a delicious topping for sandwiches, salads, wraps, or enjoy it on its own as a flavorful snack.

This BBQ tempeh bacon is savory, smoky, and slightly sweet, making it a versatile and delicious vegan alternative to traditional bacon. Enjoy its crispy texture and bold flavor in your favorite dishes!

Grilled Zucchini with BBQ Rub

Ingredients:

- 2 medium zucchinis
- 2 tablespoons olive oil
- BBQ Rub (you can use store-bought or make your own with a combination of smoked paprika, garlic powder, onion powder, brown sugar, salt, pepper, and any other desired spices)

Instructions:

Preheat your grill to medium-high heat.
Wash the zucchinis and trim off the ends. Cut them lengthwise into slices about 1/4 inch thick.
In a small bowl, mix together the olive oil and BBQ rub to create a paste.
Brush both sides of the zucchini slices with the olive oil and BBQ rub mixture, ensuring they are evenly coated.
Place the zucchini slices directly on the preheated grill grates.
Grill the zucchini slices for about 3-4 minutes on each side, or until they are tender and have grill marks.
Once cooked through, remove the grilled zucchini slices from the grill and transfer them to a serving platter.
Serve the Grilled Zucchini with BBQ Rub hot as a delicious side dish for your barbecue or meal.

This Grilled Zucchini with BBQ Rub is flavorful and easy to make, perfect for summer cookouts or as a tasty side dish any time of the year. Adjust the amount of BBQ rub according to your taste preferences. Enjoy!

Vegan BBQ Pulled Mushroom Sandwiches

Ingredients:

- 4 large portobello mushrooms, stems removed
- 1 tablespoon olive oil
- 1 onion, finely chopped
- 2 cloves garlic, minced
- 1 cup barbecue sauce (ensure it's vegan)
- 2 tablespoons soy sauce or tamari
- 1 tablespoon maple syrup or agave nectar
- 1 tablespoon apple cider vinegar
- 1 teaspoon smoked paprika
- Salt and pepper to taste
- Hamburger buns or sandwich rolls
- Optional toppings: coleslaw, pickles, sliced onions, etc.

Instructions:

Heat the olive oil in a large skillet over medium heat. Add the chopped onion and minced garlic, and sauté until softened, about 3-4 minutes.
Slice the portobello mushrooms into thin strips and add them to the skillet. Cook for about 5-7 minutes, stirring occasionally, until the mushrooms are tender and browned.
In a small bowl, whisk together the barbecue sauce, soy sauce or tamari, maple syrup or agave nectar, apple cider vinegar, smoked paprika, salt, and pepper.
Pour the barbecue sauce mixture over the cooked mushrooms in the skillet. Stir to coat the mushrooms evenly.
Reduce the heat to low and simmer the mushroom mixture for 5-7 minutes, stirring occasionally, until the sauce is thickened and the flavors are well combined.
While the mushrooms are simmering, toast the hamburger buns or sandwich rolls if desired.
Once the mushroom mixture is ready, spoon it onto the bottom halves of the hamburger buns or sandwich rolls.
Add your desired toppings, such as coleslaw, pickles, sliced onions, etc.
Place the top halves of the hamburger buns or sandwich rolls over the filling to complete the sandwiches.

Serve the Vegan BBQ Pulled Mushroom Sandwiches hot and enjoy!

These sandwiches are savory, smoky, and satisfying, making them a perfect vegan alternative to traditional pulled pork sandwiches. Feel free to customize the toppings and adjust the seasonings to suit your taste preferences. Enjoy!

BBQ Portobello Mushroom Steaks

Ingredients:

- 4 large portobello mushrooms, stems removed
- 1/4 cup balsamic vinegar
- 2 tablespoons olive oil
- 2 cloves garlic, minced
- 1 teaspoon dried thyme
- Salt and pepper to taste
- 1 cup barbecue sauce (ensure it's vegan)
- Optional toppings: sliced red onions, chopped parsley, avocado slices, etc.

Instructions:

In a shallow dish, whisk together balsamic vinegar, olive oil, minced garlic, dried thyme, salt, and pepper to create a marinade.
Place the portobello mushrooms in the marinade, turning to coat each side. Let them marinate for at least 20-30 minutes, flipping halfway through if possible.
Preheat your grill to medium-high heat.
Remove the mushrooms from the marinade and shake off any excess. Reserve the marinade for basting.
Place the mushrooms on the preheated grill, gill side down. Grill for about 4-5 minutes on each side, or until they are tender and have grill marks.
While the mushrooms are grilling, you can heat the barbecue sauce in a small saucepan over medium heat until warmed through.
Brush the grilled mushrooms with barbecue sauce occasionally while grilling to add flavor.
Once the mushrooms are cooked through, remove them from the grill and transfer them to a serving platter.
Serve the BBQ Portobello Mushroom Steaks hot, topped with any optional toppings you desire.
Enjoy your delicious barbecue portobello mushroom steaks!

These mushroom steaks are hearty and flavorful, making them a satisfying vegan option for your barbecue. Feel free to customize the toppings and adjust the seasonings to suit your taste preferences. Enjoy!

Grilled Tofu Skewers with BBQ Marinade

Ingredients:

- 1 block (14-16 oz) extra-firm tofu, pressed and drained
- Wooden or metal skewers
- For the BBQ Marinade:
    - 1/4 cup barbecue sauce (ensure it's vegan)
    - 2 tablespoons soy sauce or tamari
    - 2 tablespoons maple syrup or agave nectar
    - 2 tablespoons olive oil
    - 2 cloves garlic, minced
    - 1 teaspoon smoked paprika
    - Salt and pepper to taste
- Optional vegetables for skewering: bell peppers, onions, cherry tomatoes, zucchini, mushrooms, etc.

Instructions:

If using wooden skewers, soak them in water for at least 30 minutes to prevent burning.

Cut the pressed and drained tofu into cubes.

In a mixing bowl, whisk together all the ingredients for the BBQ marinade until well combined.

Place the tofu cubes in the marinade, ensuring they are evenly coated. Allow them to marinate for at least 30 minutes, or longer for more flavor, in the refrigerator.

Preheat your grill to medium-high heat.

If using vegetables, chop them into bite-sized pieces.

Thread the marinated tofu cubes (and vegetables, if using) onto the skewers, alternating between tofu and vegetables.

Lightly oil the grill grates to prevent sticking.

Place the tofu skewers on the preheated grill and cook for about 10-12 minutes, turning occasionally, until the tofu is lightly charred and cooked through.

While grilling, you can brush some extra marinade onto the skewers for added flavor.

Once cooked, remove the tofu skewers from the grill and transfer them to a serving platter.

Serve the Grilled Tofu Skewers with BBQ Marinade hot, garnished with chopped fresh herbs if desired.
Enjoy your delicious barbecue tofu skewers as a main dish or alongside your favorite side dishes!

These tofu skewers are packed with flavor and make for a satisfying vegan barbecue option. Feel free to customize the vegetables and adjust the seasonings to suit your taste preferences. Enjoy!

Vegan BBQ Meatballs

Ingredients:

For the Meatballs:

- 1 can (15 oz) chickpeas, drained and rinsed
- 1 cup cooked brown rice
- 1/2 cup breadcrumbs (ensure they're vegan)
- 1/4 cup finely chopped onion
- 2 cloves garlic, minced
- 2 tablespoons tomato paste
- 1 tablespoon soy sauce or tamari
- 1 tablespoon nutritional yeast
- 1 teaspoon smoked paprika
- 1/2 teaspoon ground cumin
- Salt and pepper to taste

For the BBQ Sauce:

- 1 cup barbecue sauce (ensure it's vegan)
- 2 tablespoons maple syrup or agave nectar
- 1 tablespoon apple cider vinegar
- 1 teaspoon smoked paprika
- 1/2 teaspoon garlic powder
- Salt and pepper to taste

Instructions:

Preheat your oven to 375°F (190°C). Line a baking sheet with parchment paper or lightly grease it.

In a food processor, combine the chickpeas, cooked brown rice, breadcrumbs, chopped onion, minced garlic, tomato paste, soy sauce or tamari, nutritional yeast, smoked paprika, ground cumin, salt, and pepper. Pulse until the mixture comes together but is still slightly chunky.

Roll the mixture into balls, about 1 inch in diameter, and place them on the prepared baking sheet.

Bake the meatballs in the preheated oven for 20-25 minutes, or until they are firm and lightly browned.

While the meatballs are baking, prepare the BBQ sauce. In a small saucepan, combine the barbecue sauce, maple syrup or agave nectar, apple cider vinegar, smoked paprika, garlic powder, salt, and pepper. Heat over medium heat, stirring occasionally, until warmed through and well combined.

Once the meatballs are done baking, transfer them to a large bowl and pour the BBQ sauce over them. Gently toss until the meatballs are evenly coated with the sauce.

Serve the Vegan BBQ Meatballs hot as an appetizer, main dish, or as part of a meal with your favorite sides.

These vegan BBQ meatballs are flavorful, hearty, and perfect for serving at gatherings or enjoying as a satisfying meal. Feel free to adjust the seasonings and sauce to suit your taste preferences. Enjoy!

BBQ Chickpea Stuffed Bell Peppers

Ingredients:

- 4 large bell peppers, any color
- 1 can (15 oz) chickpeas, drained and rinsed
- 1 cup cooked quinoa or rice
- 1/2 cup barbecue sauce (ensure it's vegan)
- 1/2 cup diced onion
- 1/2 cup diced bell pepper (from tops of the bell peppers)
- 2 cloves garlic, minced
- 1 teaspoon olive oil
- 1 teaspoon smoked paprika
- 1/2 teaspoon ground cumin
- Salt and pepper to taste
- Optional toppings: sliced avocado, chopped cilantro, vegan cheese, etc.

Instructions:

Preheat your oven to 375°F (190°C). Lightly grease a baking dish large enough to hold the stuffed bell peppers.

Slice the tops off the bell peppers and remove the seeds and membranes. Dice the flesh from the tops of the bell peppers and set aside.

Heat olive oil in a large skillet over medium heat. Add diced onion, diced bell pepper, and minced garlic. Cook until softened, about 5 minutes.

Add chickpeas to the skillet and cook for another 3-4 minutes, mashing some of the chickpeas with a fork or potato masher.

Stir in cooked quinoa or rice, barbecue sauce, smoked paprika, ground cumin, salt, and pepper. Cook for another 2-3 minutes, until heated through.

Stuff each bell pepper with the chickpea mixture, pressing down gently to pack it in.

Place the stuffed bell peppers in the prepared baking dish.

Cover the dish with aluminum foil and bake in the preheated oven for 30-35 minutes, or until the bell peppers are tender.

Remove the foil and bake for an additional 5-10 minutes, or until the tops are slightly browned.

Once cooked, remove the stuffed bell peppers from the oven and let them cool for a few minutes before serving.

Serve the BBQ Chickpea Stuffed Bell Peppers hot, garnished with your favorite toppings such as sliced avocado, chopped cilantro, or vegan cheese.

These BBQ chickpea stuffed bell peppers are flavorful, nutritious, and easy to make. They make a satisfying main dish for lunch or dinner, and you can customize the toppings according to your taste preferences. Enjoy!

Grilled Eggplant with BBQ Sauce

Ingredients:

- 1 large eggplant, sliced into rounds or lengthwise
- Olive oil
- Salt and pepper to taste
- BBQ sauce (ensure it's vegan)

Instructions:

Preheat your grill to medium-high heat.
Brush both sides of the eggplant slices with olive oil and season with salt and pepper.
Place the eggplant slices on the preheated grill and cook for about 3-4 minutes on each side, or until they are tender and grill marks appear.
Brush one side of the grilled eggplant slices with BBQ sauce.
Flip the eggplant slices and brush the other side with BBQ sauce as well.
Continue grilling for another 1-2 minutes on each side, allowing the BBQ sauce to caramelize slightly.
Once cooked through and caramelized, remove the grilled eggplant slices from the grill and transfer them to a serving platter.
Serve the Grilled Eggplant with BBQ Sauce hot as a side dish or appetizer.

This grilled eggplant with BBQ sauce is simple to make and packed with flavor. It's a perfect addition to your summer barbecue or as a tasty side dish any time of the year. Enjoy!

Vegan BBQ Cauliflower Steaks

Ingredients:

- 1 large head cauliflower
- Olive oil
- Salt and pepper to taste
- BBQ sauce (ensure it's vegan)
- Optional: additional seasonings such as smoked paprika, garlic powder, or onion powder

Instructions:

Preheat your oven to 425°F (220°C). Line a baking sheet with parchment paper or lightly grease it.
Remove the leaves from the cauliflower head and trim the stem end so it sits flat on the cutting board.
Slice the cauliflower into 1-inch thick slices, starting from the center of the cauliflower head and working outward. These slices are your cauliflower steaks.
Place the cauliflower steaks on the prepared baking sheet.
Brush both sides of the cauliflower steaks with olive oil and season with salt and pepper. If desired, sprinkle additional seasonings such as smoked paprika, garlic powder, or onion powder on top.
Bake the cauliflower steaks in the preheated oven for 20-25 minutes, flipping halfway through, or until they are tender and golden brown.
Once the cauliflower steaks are cooked, remove them from the oven and brush one side with BBQ sauce.
Flip the cauliflower steaks and brush the other side with BBQ sauce as well.
Return the cauliflower steaks to the oven and bake for an additional 5-10 minutes, allowing the BBQ sauce to caramelize slightly.
Once cooked through and caramelized, remove the cauliflower steaks from the oven and transfer them to a serving platter.
Serve the Vegan BBQ Cauliflower Steaks hot as a main dish or alongside your favorite side dishes.

These BBQ cauliflower steaks are flavorful, satisfying, and make for a delicious vegan alternative to traditional steak. They're perfect for serving at summer barbecues or as a tasty weeknight dinner option. Enjoy!

BBQ Black Bean Burgers

Ingredients:

- 2 cans (15 ounces each) black beans, drained and rinsed
- 1 cup cooked quinoa or brown rice
- 1/2 cup breadcrumbs (ensure they're vegan)
- 1/4 cup finely chopped onion
- 2 cloves garlic, minced
- 2 tablespoons barbecue sauce (ensure it's vegan), plus extra for serving
- 1 tablespoon soy sauce or tamari
- 1 tablespoon ground flaxseed meal + 3 tablespoons water (or use a flax egg)
- 1 teaspoon smoked paprika
- 1/2 teaspoon ground cumin
- Salt and pepper to taste
- Olive oil or cooking spray for frying
- Burger buns and toppings of choice (lettuce, tomato, avocado, vegan cheese, etc.)

Instructions:

In a small bowl, mix together the ground flaxseed meal and water. Let it sit for 5-10 minutes to thicken and form a flax egg.

In a large mixing bowl, mash the black beans with a fork or potato masher until they are mostly mashed but still have some texture.

Add the cooked quinoa or brown rice, breadcrumbs, chopped onion, minced garlic, barbecue sauce, soy sauce or tamari, ground flaxseed mixture (or flax egg), smoked paprika, ground cumin, salt, and pepper to the mashed black beans. Mix until well combined.

Divide the mixture into 4 equal portions and shape each portion into a burger patty.

Heat a skillet over medium heat and lightly coat it with olive oil or cooking spray. Place the black bean burger patties in the skillet and cook for 4-5 minutes on each side, or until golden brown and heated through.

While the burgers are cooking, toast the burger buns if desired.

Once the black bean burgers are cooked, assemble them on the burger buns with your favorite toppings, such as lettuce, tomato, avocado, vegan cheese, etc.

Serve the BBQ Black Bean Burgers hot, with extra barbecue sauce on the side if desired.

Enjoy your delicious and flavorful vegan barbecue black bean burgers!

These black bean burgers are hearty, flavorful, and perfect for a vegan barbecue or a quick weeknight meal. Feel free to customize the seasonings and toppings to suit your taste preferences. Enjoy!

Grilled Asparagus with BBQ Seasoning

Ingredients:

- 1 pound (about 450g) fresh asparagus spears, tough ends trimmed
- 2 tablespoons olive oil
- BBQ seasoning mix (you can use store-bought or make your own with a combination of paprika, garlic powder, onion powder, smoked paprika, cumin, chili powder, salt, and pepper)
- Salt and pepper to taste

Instructions:

Preheat your grill to medium-high heat.
Place the trimmed asparagus spears in a large mixing bowl.
Drizzle the olive oil over the asparagus and toss until they are evenly coated.
Sprinkle the BBQ seasoning mix over the asparagus, tossing again to ensure they are evenly coated with the seasoning.
Season the asparagus with salt and pepper to taste.
Once the grill is hot, place the seasoned asparagus spears directly on the grill grates in a single layer.
Grill the asparagus for about 5-7 minutes, turning occasionally, or until they are tender and slightly charred.
Once cooked through, remove the grilled asparagus from the grill and transfer them to a serving platter.
Serve the Grilled Asparagus with BBQ Seasoning hot as a delicious side dish for your barbecue or meal.

This grilled asparagus with BBQ seasoning is flavorful, nutritious, and easy to make. It's a perfect addition to your summer cookouts or as a tasty side dish any time of the year.

Enjoy!

BBQ Seitan Skewers with Vegetables

Ingredients:

For the Seitan:

- 1 cup vital wheat gluten
- 2 tablespoons nutritional yeast
- 1 teaspoon onion powder
- 1 teaspoon garlic powder
- 1/2 teaspoon smoked paprika
- 1/2 teaspoon dried thyme
- 1/2 teaspoon dried oregano
- 3/4 cup vegetable broth
- 2 tablespoons soy sauce or tamari
- 1 tablespoon tomato paste
- 1 tablespoon olive oil
- 1 tablespoon vegan Worcestershire sauce
- 1 tablespoon liquid smoke

For the BBQ Sauce:

- 1 cup barbecue sauce (ensure it's vegan)
- 2 tablespoons apple cider vinegar
- 1 tablespoon maple syrup or agave nectar
- 1 tablespoon Dijon mustard
- 1 teaspoon smoked paprika
- 1/2 teaspoon garlic powder
- Salt and pepper to taste

For the Skewers:

- Seitan cubes (from the prepared seitan mixture)
- Assorted vegetables (such as bell peppers, onions, cherry tomatoes, zucchini, mushrooms, etc.)

Instructions:

In a large mixing bowl, combine the vital wheat gluten, nutritional yeast, onion powder, garlic powder, smoked paprika, dried thyme, and dried oregano.

In a separate bowl, whisk together the vegetable broth, soy sauce or tamari, tomato paste, olive oil, vegan Worcestershire sauce, and liquid smoke.

Pour the wet ingredients into the dry ingredients and mix until a dough forms.

Knead the dough for a few minutes to develop the gluten, then let it rest for about 5 minutes.

Divide the seitan dough into cubes and thread them onto skewers alternately with the assorted vegetables.

In a small bowl, mix together all the ingredients for the BBQ sauce until well combined.

Preheat your grill to medium-high heat.

Brush the skewers with some of the BBQ sauce, reserving the rest for basting.

Place the skewers on the preheated grill and cook for about 10-12 minutes, turning occasionally and basting with the remaining BBQ sauce, until the seitan is browned and the vegetables are tender.

Once cooked through, remove the skewers from the grill and transfer them to a serving platter.

Serve the BBQ Seitan Skewers with Vegetables hot, garnished with chopped fresh herbs if desired.

These BBQ seitan skewers with vegetables are savory, smoky, and perfect for grilling season. Enjoy them as a main dish or as part of a barbecue spread. Feel free to customize the vegetables and adjust the seasoning according to your taste preferences. Enjoy!

Vegan BBQ Jackfruit Tacos

Ingredients:

For the BBQ Jackfruit:

- 2 cans (20 oz each) young green jackfruit in brine or water, drained and rinsed
- 1 tablespoon olive oil
- 1/2 onion, finely chopped
- 2 cloves garlic, minced
- 1/2 cup barbecue sauce (ensure it's vegan)
- 1/4 cup vegetable broth or water
- 1 tablespoon soy sauce or tamari
- 1 tablespoon maple syrup or agave nectar
- 1 teaspoon smoked paprika
- 1/2 teaspoon garlic powder
- 1/2 teaspoon onion powder
- Salt and pepper to taste

For the Tacos:

- 8 small corn tortillas
- BBQ Jackfruit mixture
- Optional toppings: shredded lettuce, diced tomatoes, sliced avocado, chopped cilantro, lime wedges, vegan cheese, etc.

Instructions:

Heat the olive oil in a large skillet over medium heat. Add the chopped onion and minced garlic, and cook until softened and fragrant, about 2-3 minutes.
Add the drained and rinsed jackfruit to the skillet. Use a potato masher or fork to break up the jackfruit into smaller pieces.
In a small bowl, whisk together the barbecue sauce, vegetable broth or water, soy sauce or tamari, maple syrup or agave nectar, smoked paprika, garlic powder, onion powder, salt, and pepper.
Pour the barbecue sauce mixture over the jackfruit in the skillet and stir to combine. Cook for about 10-15 minutes, stirring occasionally, until the jackfruit is tender and the sauce has thickened.

While the jackfruit mixture is cooking, warm the corn tortillas in a separate skillet or on a grill until heated through.

Once the jackfruit mixture is cooked, assemble the tacos by spooning some of the BBQ jackfruit onto each tortilla.

Add your desired toppings, such as shredded lettuce, diced tomatoes, sliced avocado, chopped cilantro, lime wedges, vegan cheese, etc.

Serve the Vegan BBQ Jackfruit Tacos hot, with extra barbecue sauce on the side if desired.

These vegan BBQ jackfruit tacos are savory, smoky, and packed with flavor. They're perfect for a quick and easy weeknight dinner or for serving at gatherings. Customize the toppings to suit your taste preferences and enjoy!

BBQ Sweet Potato Wedges

Ingredients:

- 2 large sweet potatoes, scrubbed and cut into wedges
- 2 tablespoons olive oil
- 1 tablespoon smoked paprika
- 1 teaspoon garlic powder
- 1 teaspoon onion powder
- 1 teaspoon ground cumin
- 1/2 teaspoon chili powder
- Salt and pepper to taste
- 1/4 cup barbecue sauce (ensure it's vegan)
- Optional garnish: chopped fresh cilantro or parsley

Instructions:

Preheat your oven to 425°F (220°C). Line a baking sheet with parchment paper or aluminum foil.

In a large bowl, toss the sweet potato wedges with olive oil, smoked paprika, garlic powder, onion powder, ground cumin, chili powder, salt, and pepper until evenly coated.

Spread the seasoned sweet potato wedges out in a single layer on the prepared baking sheet.

Bake in the preheated oven for 20-25 minutes, flipping halfway through, or until the sweet potato wedges are tender and golden brown.

Remove the baking sheet from the oven and brush the sweet potato wedges with barbecue sauce.

Return the baking sheet to the oven and bake for an additional 5-10 minutes, or until the barbecue sauce is caramelized and sticky.

Once cooked through and caramelized, remove the BBQ sweet potato wedges from the oven.

Optional: Garnish with chopped fresh cilantro or parsley before serving.

Serve the BBQ Sweet Potato Wedges hot as a delicious side dish or appetizer.

These BBQ sweet potato wedges are flavorful, crispy, and make a perfect side dish for any barbecue or gathering. Enjoy!

Grilled Avocado with BBQ Drizzle

Ingredients:

- 2 ripe avocados
- Olive oil
- Salt and pepper to taste
- BBQ sauce (ensure it's vegan)
- Optional garnish: chopped cilantro, sliced green onions, or red pepper flakes

Instructions:

Preheat your grill to medium-high heat.
Cut the avocados in half lengthwise and remove the pits.
Brush the cut sides of the avocado halves lightly with olive oil to prevent sticking.
Season the cut sides of the avocado halves with salt and pepper to taste.
Place the avocado halves, cut side down, directly onto the grill grates.
Grill the avocados for 2-3 minutes, or until grill marks appear and the avocados are slightly softened.
Carefully remove the grilled avocado halves from the grill and place them on a serving platter, cut side up.
Drizzle the grilled avocado halves with BBQ sauce.
Optional: Garnish with chopped cilantro, sliced green onions, or red pepper flakes for added flavor and color.
Serve the Grilled Avocado with BBQ Drizzle immediately as a tasty appetizer or side dish.

These grilled avocados with BBQ drizzle are a flavorful and unique addition to any barbecue or summer gathering. Enjoy the creamy texture of the grilled avocado paired with the sweet and smoky flavor of the barbecue sauce.

Vegan BBQ Beans

Ingredients:

- 2 cans (15 oz each) of your favorite beans (such as black beans, kidney beans, or pinto beans), drained and rinsed
- 1 tablespoon olive oil
- 1/2 onion, finely chopped
- 2 cloves garlic, minced
- 1/2 cup barbecue sauce (ensure it's vegan)
- 1/4 cup vegetable broth or water
- 2 tablespoons tomato paste
- 1 tablespoon maple syrup or agave nectar
- 1 teaspoon smoked paprika
- 1/2 teaspoon ground cumin
- Salt and pepper to taste
- Optional: chopped fresh cilantro or green onions for garnish

Instructions:

Heat the olive oil in a large skillet over medium heat.
Add the chopped onion and minced garlic to the skillet. Cook until the onion is softened and translucent, about 2-3 minutes.
Stir in the drained and rinsed beans, barbecue sauce, vegetable broth or water, tomato paste, maple syrup or agave nectar, smoked paprika, ground cumin, salt, and pepper.
Bring the mixture to a simmer, then reduce the heat to low. Let it simmer for 10-15 minutes, stirring occasionally, until the beans are heated through and the flavors have melded together.
Taste and adjust the seasonings as needed, adding more salt, pepper, or barbecue sauce if desired.
Once the beans are cooked to your liking, remove the skillet from the heat.
Transfer the Vegan BBQ Beans to a serving dish and garnish with chopped fresh cilantro or green onions if desired.
Serve the Vegan BBQ Beans hot as a side dish or main course.

These Vegan BBQ Beans are flavorful, hearty, and perfect for serving at barbecues, picnics, or as a comforting weeknight meal. Enjoy!

BBQ Tempeh Sliders

Ingredients:

- 1 package (8 oz) tempeh, sliced into 1/4-inch thick pieces
- 1/4 cup barbecue sauce (ensure it's vegan), plus extra for serving
- 1 tablespoon soy sauce or tamari
- 1 tablespoon olive oil
- 1 clove garlic, minced
- 1 teaspoon smoked paprika
- 1/2 teaspoon onion powder
- 1/4 teaspoon garlic powder
- Pinch of cayenne pepper (optional)
- Slider buns
- Optional toppings: sliced tomatoes, lettuce, pickles, vegan cheese, etc.

Instructions:

In a small bowl, whisk together the barbecue sauce, soy sauce or tamari, olive oil, minced garlic, smoked paprika, onion powder, garlic powder, and cayenne pepper (if using).
Place the tempeh slices in a shallow dish or a resealable plastic bag. Pour the marinade over the tempeh slices, making sure they are evenly coated. Marinate for at least 30 minutes, or up to overnight in the refrigerator.
Preheat your grill or grill pan over medium-high heat.
Remove the tempeh slices from the marinade, shaking off any excess marinade. Grill the tempeh slices for 3-4 minutes on each side, or until they are lightly charred and heated through.
Assemble the sliders by placing a grilled tempeh slice on the bottom half of each slider bun.
Top the tempeh slices with additional barbecue sauce and your choice of toppings, such as sliced tomatoes, lettuce, pickles, vegan cheese, etc.
Place the top half of the slider buns on top of the toppings to complete the sliders.
Serve the BBQ Tempeh Sliders immediately, and enjoy!

These BBQ Tempeh Sliders are savory, smoky, and perfect for serving at parties, cookouts, or as a quick and tasty meal. Customize the toppings according to your taste preferences, and enjoy the delicious flavors of barbecue tempeh!

Grilled Portobello Mushroom Fajitas with BBQ Sauce

Ingredients:

- 4 large portobello mushrooms, stems removed
- 2 bell peppers, sliced
- 1 onion, sliced
- 2 tablespoons olive oil
- 1 teaspoon chili powder
- 1 teaspoon smoked paprika
- 1/2 teaspoon ground cumin
- Salt and pepper to taste
- 8 small tortillas (corn or flour)
- BBQ sauce (ensure it's vegan)
- Optional toppings: sliced avocado, chopped cilantro, vegan sour cream, lime wedges, etc.

Instructions:

Preheat your grill to medium-high heat.
In a small bowl, mix together the olive oil, chili powder, smoked paprika, ground cumin, salt, and pepper to create a marinade.
Brush both sides of the portobello mushrooms, bell peppers, and onion slices with the marinade.
Place the portobello mushrooms, bell peppers, and onions on the preheated grill. Cook for about 4-5 minutes per side, or until they are tender and have grill marks.
While the vegetables are grilling, warm the tortillas on the grill or in a skillet until they are soft and pliable.
Once the vegetables are cooked, remove them from the grill and slice the portobello mushrooms into strips.
Assemble the fajitas by placing some sliced portobello mushrooms, bell peppers, and onions onto each tortilla.
Drizzle some BBQ sauce over the vegetables.
Add your desired toppings, such as sliced avocado, chopped cilantro, vegan sour cream, or a squeeze of lime juice.
Serve the Grilled Portobello Mushroom Fajitas with BBQ Sauce hot, and enjoy!

These Grilled Portobello Mushroom Fajitas with BBQ Sauce are flavorful, filling, and perfect for a vegan-friendly meal. Feel free to customize the toppings and adjust the seasonings to suit your taste preferences. Enjoy!

BBQ Tofu Nuggets

Ingredients:

- 1 block (14-16 oz) extra-firm tofu, pressed and drained
- 1/2 cup barbecue sauce (ensure it's vegan)
- 2 tablespoons soy sauce or tamari
- 2 tablespoons maple syrup or agave nectar
- 1 tablespoon olive oil
- 1 teaspoon smoked paprika
- 1/2 teaspoon garlic powder
- 1/2 teaspoon onion powder
- Salt and pepper to taste
- 1 cup breadcrumbs (ensure they're vegan)
- Cooking spray or oil for greasing

Instructions:

Preheat your oven to 400°F (200°C). Line a baking sheet with parchment paper or lightly grease it.
Cut the pressed and drained tofu into small nugget-sized pieces.
In a shallow dish, whisk together the barbecue sauce, soy sauce or tamari, maple syrup or agave nectar, olive oil, smoked paprika, garlic powder, onion powder, salt, and pepper to create the marinade.
Place the tofu nuggets in the marinade, turning to coat each piece evenly. Let them marinate for at least 15-20 minutes.
Place the breadcrumbs in another shallow dish.
Remove each tofu nugget from the marinade, allowing any excess marinade to drip off, and then coat it in breadcrumbs, pressing gently to adhere.
Place the breaded tofu nuggets on the prepared baking sheet in a single layer. Lightly spray or brush the tops of the tofu nuggets with cooking spray or oil to help them crisp up.
Bake in the preheated oven for 20-25 minutes, flipping halfway through, or until the tofu nuggets are golden brown and crispy.
Once cooked through, remove the BBQ Tofu Nuggets from the oven and let them cool for a few minutes before serving.
Serve the BBQ Tofu Nuggets hot as a delicious appetizer or main dish, alongside your favorite dipping sauce or with sides like fries or salad.

These BBQ Tofu Nuggets are crispy, flavorful, and perfect for satisfying your craving for a tasty snack or meal. Enjoy!

Vegan BBQ Stuffed Bell Peppers

Ingredients:

- 4 large bell peppers, any color
- 1 cup cooked quinoa or rice
- 1 cup canned black beans, drained and rinsed
- 1 cup corn kernels (fresh, canned, or frozen)
- 1/2 cup diced onion
- 1/2 cup diced tomatoes
- 1/2 cup barbecue sauce (ensure it's vegan)
- 1 tablespoon olive oil
- 1 teaspoon chili powder
- 1/2 teaspoon smoked paprika
- Salt and pepper to taste
- Optional toppings: chopped fresh cilantro, sliced avocado, vegan cheese, etc.

Instructions:

Preheat your oven to 375°F (190°C). Grease a baking dish large enough to hold the stuffed bell peppers.
Cut the tops off the bell peppers and remove the seeds and membranes. Place the hollowed-out bell peppers in the prepared baking dish, cut side up.
In a large skillet, heat the olive oil over medium heat. Add the diced onion and cook until softened, about 3-4 minutes.
Add the diced tomatoes, cooked quinoa or rice, black beans, corn kernels, barbecue sauce, chili powder, smoked paprika, salt, and pepper to the skillet. Stir to combine and cook for another 3-4 minutes, until heated through.
Spoon the quinoa and bean mixture into each bell pepper until they are full and slightly overflowing.
Cover the baking dish with aluminum foil and bake in the preheated oven for 25-30 minutes, or until the bell peppers are tender.
Remove the foil and bake for an additional 5-10 minutes, or until the tops are slightly browned.
Once cooked through, remove the stuffed bell peppers from the oven and let them cool for a few minutes before serving.
Garnish the Vegan BBQ Stuffed Bell Peppers with optional toppings such as chopped fresh cilantro, sliced avocado, or vegan cheese if desired.
Serve the stuffed bell peppers hot as a delicious and satisfying main dish.

These Vegan BBQ Stuffed Bell Peppers are hearty, flavorful, and packed with protein and nutrients. They make for a delicious and wholesome meal that's perfect for lunch or dinner. Enjoy!

Grilled Pineapple and Avocado Salad with BBQ Dressing

Ingredients:

For the Salad:

- 1 small pineapple, peeled, cored, and sliced into rings
- 2 ripe avocados, peeled, pitted, and sliced
- 4 cups mixed salad greens (such as baby spinach, arugula, or lettuce)
- 1/4 cup red onion, thinly sliced
- 1/4 cup chopped fresh cilantro or parsley
- Optional: toasted nuts or seeds for added crunch

For the BBQ Dressing:

- 1/4 cup barbecue sauce (ensure it's vegan)
- 2 tablespoons olive oil
- 1 tablespoon apple cider vinegar
- 1 teaspoon Dijon mustard
- 1 teaspoon maple syrup or agave nectar
- Salt and pepper to taste

Instructions:

Preheat your grill or grill pan to medium-high heat.
Place the pineapple slices on the preheated grill and cook for 2-3 minutes on each side, or until grill marks appear and the pineapple is slightly caramelized. Remove from the grill and set aside.
In a small bowl, whisk together all the ingredients for the BBQ dressing until well combined. Adjust the seasoning to taste, adding more salt, pepper, or sweetener if desired.
In a large salad bowl, combine the mixed salad greens, sliced avocado, grilled pineapple slices, thinly sliced red onion, and chopped fresh cilantro or parsley.
Drizzle the BBQ dressing over the salad and toss gently to coat all the ingredients evenly.
Optional: Sprinkle toasted nuts or seeds over the salad for added crunch and texture.

Serve the Grilled Pineapple and Avocado Salad with BBQ Dressing immediately as a refreshing and flavorful side dish or light meal.

This Grilled Pineapple and Avocado Salad with BBQ Dressing is bursting with sweet, tangy, and smoky flavors. It's perfect for summer gatherings, barbecues, or as a healthy weeknight dinner option. Enjoy!

BBQ Cauliflower Tacos

Ingredients:

For the BBQ Cauliflower:

- 1 head cauliflower, cut into florets
- 2 tablespoons olive oil
- 1/2 cup barbecue sauce (ensure it's vegan)
- 1 tablespoon soy sauce or tamari
- 1 teaspoon smoked paprika
- 1/2 teaspoon garlic powder
- 1/2 teaspoon onion powder
- Salt and pepper to taste

For the Tacos:

- 8 small tortillas (corn or flour)
- BBQ Cauliflower
- Coleslaw or shredded cabbage
- Sliced avocado
- Chopped cilantro
- Lime wedges
- Optional toppings: diced tomatoes, sliced jalapeños, vegan cheese, etc.

Instructions:

Preheat your oven to 425°F (220°C). Line a baking sheet with parchment paper or lightly grease it.
In a large bowl, toss the cauliflower florets with olive oil, smoked paprika, garlic powder, onion powder, salt, and pepper until evenly coated.
Spread the seasoned cauliflower florets out in a single layer on the prepared baking sheet.
Roast the cauliflower in the preheated oven for 20-25 minutes, flipping halfway through, or until the cauliflower is tender and caramelized.
While the cauliflower is roasting, prepare the BBQ sauce by mixing together the barbecue sauce and soy sauce or tamari in a small bowl.
Once the cauliflower is cooked, transfer it to a large mixing bowl and toss it with the BBQ sauce mixture until evenly coated.

Warm the tortillas in a skillet or microwave until heated through.

Assemble the tacos by placing a generous portion of BBQ cauliflower onto each tortilla.

Top the BBQ cauliflower with coleslaw or shredded cabbage, sliced avocado, chopped cilantro, and any other desired toppings.

Serve the BBQ Cauliflower Tacos hot, with lime wedges on the side for squeezing over the tacos.

These BBQ Cauliflower Tacos are flavorful, filling, and perfect for a vegan-friendly meal. Customize the toppings to suit your taste preferences, and enjoy the delicious combination of smoky cauliflower and tangy barbecue sauce!

Vegan BBQ Slaw

Ingredients:

For the Slaw:

- 4 cups shredded cabbage (green or purple cabbage, or a mix)
- 1 cup shredded carrots
- 1/4 cup chopped fresh cilantro
- 1/4 cup chopped green onions (optional)
- 1/4 cup chopped red onion (optional)
- 1/4 cup chopped bell pepper (optional)

For the Dressing:

- 1/2 cup vegan mayonnaise
- 2 tablespoons barbecue sauce (ensure it's vegan)
- 1 tablespoon apple cider vinegar
- 1 tablespoon maple syrup or agave nectar
- 1 teaspoon Dijon mustard
- Salt and pepper to taste

Instructions:

> In a large mixing bowl, combine the shredded cabbage, shredded carrots, chopped cilantro, and any optional vegetables you're using (such as green onions, red onion, or bell pepper).
> In a separate small bowl, whisk together the vegan mayonnaise, barbecue sauce, apple cider vinegar, maple syrup or agave nectar, Dijon mustard, salt, and pepper until well combined.
> Pour the dressing over the cabbage mixture and toss until everything is evenly coated with the dressing.
> Taste and adjust the seasoning, adding more salt, pepper, or barbecue sauce if desired.
> Cover the bowl with plastic wrap or a lid and refrigerate for at least 30 minutes to allow the flavors to meld together.
> Before serving, give the Vegan BBQ Slaw a final toss and adjust the seasoning if necessary.

Serve the Vegan BBQ Slaw cold as a refreshing and flavorful side dish alongside your favorite barbecue dishes or as a topping for sandwiches, wraps, or tacos.

This Vegan BBQ Slaw is creamy, tangy, and packed with crunchy vegetables, making it the perfect accompaniment to any barbecue or summer meal. Enjoy!

Grilled Watermelon with BBQ Rub

Ingredients:

- 1 small seedless watermelon, sliced into wedges or cubes
- BBQ rub seasoning (store-bought or homemade)
- Olive oil or cooking spray

Instructions:

Preheat your grill to medium-high heat.
Brush the watermelon slices or cubes lightly with olive oil or spray them with cooking spray to prevent sticking.
Sprinkle the BBQ rub seasoning evenly over the watermelon slices or cubes, coating them on all sides.
Once the grill is hot, place the seasoned watermelon slices or cubes directly onto the grill grates.
Grill the watermelon for about 2-3 minutes on each side, or until grill marks form and the watermelon is slightly caramelized.
Carefully remove the grilled watermelon from the grill and transfer it to a serving platter.
Serve the Grilled Watermelon with BBQ Rub immediately as a unique and flavorful appetizer or side dish.

Enjoy the combination of sweet, juicy watermelon with the savory and smoky flavors of the BBQ rub. It's a refreshing and unexpected treat that's perfect for summer cookouts and gatherings!

BBQ Seitan Sandwiches

Ingredients:

For the Seitan:

- 2 cups vital wheat gluten
- 1/4 cup nutritional yeast
- 1 teaspoon garlic powder
- 1 teaspoon onion powder
- 1 teaspoon smoked paprika
- 1 teaspoon dried thyme
- 1 teaspoon dried oregano
- 1 1/4 cups vegetable broth
- 2 tablespoons soy sauce or tamari
- 1 tablespoon olive oil
- 1 tablespoon tomato paste
- 1 tablespoon vegan Worcestershire sauce
- 1 tablespoon liquid smoke

For the BBQ Sauce:

- 1 cup barbecue sauce (ensure it's vegan)
- 2 tablespoons apple cider vinegar
- 1 tablespoon maple syrup or agave nectar
- 1 tablespoon Dijon mustard
- 1 teaspoon smoked paprika
- 1/2 teaspoon garlic powder
- Salt and pepper to taste

For the Sandwiches:

- Seitan slices
- BBQ sauce
- Sandwich buns
- Optional toppings: sliced tomatoes, lettuce, pickles, sliced onions, vegan cheese, etc.

Instructions:

Preheat your oven to 350°F (175°C).

In a large mixing bowl, whisk together the vital wheat gluten, nutritional yeast, garlic powder, onion powder, smoked paprika, dried thyme, and dried oregano.

In a separate bowl, combine the vegetable broth, soy sauce or tamari, olive oil, tomato paste, vegan Worcestershire sauce, and liquid smoke.

Pour the wet ingredients into the dry ingredients and mix until a dough forms. Knead the dough for a few minutes until it becomes elastic. Shape it into a loaf.

Wrap the seitan loaf tightly in aluminum foil and place it in a baking dish.

Bake the seitan in the preheated oven for 1 hour, flipping halfway through.

While the seitan is baking, prepare the BBQ sauce by combining all the BBQ sauce ingredients in a small saucepan over medium heat. Simmer for 5-7 minutes, stirring occasionally, until the sauce is thickened.

Remove the seitan from the oven and let it cool for a few minutes. Then, slice it thinly.

Heat a skillet over medium heat and add the sliced seitan to the skillet. Pour the BBQ sauce over the seitan slices and cook for a few minutes, stirring occasionally, until the seitan is heated through and coated with the sauce.

Assemble the sandwiches by placing the BBQ seitan slices on the sandwich buns. Add your desired toppings, such as sliced tomatoes, lettuce, pickles, sliced onions, or vegan cheese.

Serve the BBQ Seitan Sandwiches hot, and enjoy!

These BBQ Seitan Sandwiches are hearty, flavorful, and perfect for a satisfying meal. Customize the toppings to suit your taste preferences and enjoy the delicious flavors of barbecue seitan!

Vegan BBQ Stuffed Potatoes

Ingredients:

For the Seitan:

- 2 cups vital wheat gluten
- 1/4 cup nutritional yeast
- 1 teaspoon garlic powder
- 1 teaspoon onion powder
- 1 teaspoon smoked paprika
- 1 teaspoon dried thyme
- 1 teaspoon dried oregano
- 1 1/4 cups vegetable broth
- 2 tablespoons soy sauce or tamari
- 1 tablespoon olive oil
- 1 tablespoon tomato paste
- 1 tablespoon vegan Worcestershire sauce
- 1 tablespoon liquid smoke

For the BBQ Sauce:

- 1 cup barbecue sauce (ensure it's vegan)
- 2 tablespoons apple cider vinegar
- 1 tablespoon maple syrup or agave nectar
- 1 tablespoon Dijon mustard
- 1 teaspoon smoked paprika
- 1/2 teaspoon garlic powder
- Salt and pepper to taste

For the Sandwiches:

- Seitan slices
- BBQ sauce
- Sandwich buns
- Optional toppings: sliced tomatoes, lettuce, pickles, sliced onions, vegan cheese, etc.

Instructions:

1. Preheat your oven to 350°F (175°C).
2. In a large mixing bowl, whisk together the vital wheat gluten, nutritional yeast, garlic powder, onion powder, smoked paprika, dried thyme, and dried oregano.
3. In a separate bowl, combine the vegetable broth, soy sauce or tamari, olive oil, tomato paste, vegan Worcestershire sauce, and liquid smoke.
4. Pour the wet ingredients into the dry ingredients and mix until a dough forms.
5. Knead the dough for a few minutes until it becomes elastic. Shape it into a loaf.
6. Wrap the seitan loaf tightly in aluminum foil and place it in a baking dish.
7. Bake the seitan in the preheated oven for 1 hour, flipping halfway through.
8. While the seitan is baking, prepare the BBQ sauce by combining all the BBQ sauce ingredients in a small saucepan over medium heat. Simmer for 5-7 minutes, stirring occasionally, until the sauce is thickened.
9. Remove the seitan from the oven and let it cool for a few minutes. Then, slice it thinly.
10. Heat a skillet over medium heat and add the sliced seitan to the skillet. Pour the BBQ sauce over the seitan slices and cook for a few minutes, stirring occasionally, until the seitan is heated through and coated with the sauce.
11. Assemble the sandwiches by placing the BBQ seitan slices on the sandwich buns. Add your desired toppings, such as sliced tomatoes, lettuce, pickles, sliced onions, or vegan cheese.
12. Serve the BBQ Seitan Sandwiches hot, and enjoy!

These BBQ Seitan Sandwiches are hearty, flavorful, and perfect for a satisfying meal. Customize the toppings to suit your taste preferences and enjoy the delicious flavors of barbecue seitan!

Grilled Sweet Potato and Black Bean Salad with BBQ Dressing

Ingredients:

For the Salad:

- 2 large sweet potatoes, peeled and sliced into rounds
- 1 can (15 oz) black beans, drained and rinsed
- 1 red bell pepper, diced
- 1/4 cup red onion, finely chopped
- 2 tablespoons chopped fresh cilantro
- Salt and pepper to taste
- Cooking spray or olive oil for grilling

For the BBQ Dressing:

- 1/4 cup barbecue sauce (ensure it's vegan)
- 2 tablespoons olive oil
- 1 tablespoon apple cider vinegar
- 1 teaspoon Dijon mustard
- 1 teaspoon maple syrup or agave nectar
- 1/2 teaspoon smoked paprika
- 1/4 teaspoon garlic powder
- Salt and pepper to taste

Instructions:

Preheat your grill to medium-high heat.
In a small bowl, whisk together all the ingredients for the BBQ dressing until well combined. Set aside.
Lightly coat the sweet potato rounds with cooking spray or olive oil. Season with salt and pepper.
Place the sweet potato rounds on the preheated grill and cook for about 4-5 minutes per side, or until they are tender and have grill marks. Remove from the grill and set aside.
In a large mixing bowl, combine the grilled sweet potato rounds, black beans, diced red bell pepper, chopped red onion, and chopped cilantro.

Pour the BBQ dressing over the salad and toss gently to coat all the ingredients evenly.
Taste and adjust the seasoning, adding more salt and pepper if needed.
Serve the Grilled Sweet Potato and Black Bean Salad with BBQ Dressing immediately as a flavorful and satisfying side dish or light meal.

This Grilled Sweet Potato and Black Bean Salad with BBQ Dressing is hearty, nutritious, and bursting with flavor. Enjoy the combination of smoky grilled sweet potatoes, protein-rich black beans, and tangy barbecue dressing!

BBQ Tempeh Tacos

Ingredients:

For the BBQ Tempeh:

- 1 package (8 oz) tempeh, crumbled or sliced
- 1/2 cup barbecue sauce (ensure it's vegan)
- 2 tablespoons soy sauce or tamari
- 1 tablespoon olive oil
- 1 tablespoon maple syrup or agave nectar
- 1 teaspoon smoked paprika
- 1/2 teaspoon garlic powder
- 1/2 teaspoon onion powder
- Salt and pepper to taste

For the Tacos:

- 8 small tortillas (corn or flour)
- BBQ Tempeh
- Coleslaw or shredded cabbage
- Sliced avocado
- Chopped cilantro
- Lime wedges
- Optional toppings: diced tomatoes, sliced jalapeños, vegan cheese, etc.

Instructions:

In a small bowl, whisk together the barbecue sauce, soy sauce or tamari, olive oil, maple syrup or agave nectar, smoked paprika, garlic powder, onion powder, salt, and pepper to create the marinade.

Place the crumbled or sliced tempeh in a shallow dish or resealable plastic bag. Pour the marinade over the tempeh, making sure it's evenly coated. Let it marinate for at least 30 minutes, or longer if possible.

Preheat a skillet over medium heat. Add the marinated tempeh to the skillet and cook for 5-7 minutes, stirring occasionally, until heated through and slightly caramelized.

Warm the tortillas in a skillet or microwave until heated through.

Assemble the tacos by placing a spoonful of BBQ tempeh onto each tortilla.

Top the BBQ tempeh with coleslaw or shredded cabbage, sliced avocado, chopped cilantro, and any other desired toppings.
Serve the BBQ Tempeh Tacos hot, with lime wedges on the side for squeezing over the tacos.

These BBQ Tempeh Tacos are savory, smoky, and packed with flavor. They're perfect for a quick and satisfying meal that's sure to please vegans and non-vegans alike. Enjoy!

Vegan BBQ Jackfruit Pizza

Ingredients:

For the Pizza Dough:

- 1 pound (about 4 cups) pizza dough, store-bought or homemade
- Cornmeal or flour for dusting

For the BBQ Jackfruit Topping:

- 1 can (20 oz) young green jackfruit in brine or water, drained and rinsed
- 1/2 cup barbecue sauce (ensure it's vegan)
- 1 tablespoon olive oil
- 1/2 teaspoon smoked paprika
- 1/2 teaspoon garlic powder
- Salt and pepper to taste

For the Pizza:

- BBQ Jackfruit topping
- 1/2 cup barbecue sauce (for spreading on the pizza dough)
- 1 cup vegan cheese (shredded mozzarella or any other vegan cheese of your choice)
- 1/4 cup red onion, thinly sliced
- 2 tablespoons chopped fresh cilantro

Instructions:

Preheat your oven to 475°F (245°C). If using a pizza stone, place it in the oven while preheating.
In a small bowl, whisk together the barbecue sauce, olive oil, smoked paprika, garlic powder, salt, and pepper to create the BBQ jackfruit topping.
Using your hands or a fork, shred the jackfruit pieces to resemble pulled pork. Heat a skillet over medium heat. Add the shredded jackfruit and the prepared BBQ sauce mixture to the skillet. Cook for 5-7 minutes, stirring occasionally, until the jackfruit is heated through and coated with the sauce. Remove from heat and set aside.

Roll out the pizza dough on a lightly floured surface to your desired thickness.
If using a pizza stone, sprinkle cornmeal or flour on a pizza peel or the back of a baking sheet. Transfer the rolled-out pizza dough to the pizza peel or baking sheet.
Spread the barbecue sauce evenly over the pizza dough, leaving a small border around the edges.
Sprinkle the vegan cheese over the barbecue sauce.
Distribute the BBQ jackfruit topping evenly over the cheese.
Scatter the sliced red onion over the top of the pizza.
Carefully transfer the pizza to the preheated oven (either directly onto the pizza stone or onto a baking sheet).
Bake the pizza for 12-15 minutes, or until the crust is golden brown and the cheese is melted and bubbly.
Remove the pizza from the oven and sprinkle chopped fresh cilantro over the top.
Slice and serve the Vegan BBQ Jackfruit Pizza hot.

This Vegan BBQ Jackfruit Pizza is flavorful, satisfying, and perfect for pizza night. Enjoy the unique combination of tangy barbecue sauce, smoky jackfruit, and melty vegan cheese!

Grilled Corn and Black Bean Salad with BBQ Dressing

Ingredients:

For the Salad:

- 4 ears of corn, husked
- 1 can (15 oz) black beans, drained and rinsed
- 1 red bell pepper, diced
- 1/4 cup red onion, finely chopped
- 2 tablespoons chopped fresh cilantro
- Salt and pepper to taste
- Olive oil or cooking spray for grilling

For the BBQ Dressing:

- 1/4 cup barbecue sauce (ensure it's vegan)
- 2 tablespoons olive oil
- 1 tablespoon apple cider vinegar
- 1 tablespoon maple syrup or agave nectar
- 1 teaspoon Dijon mustard
- 1/2 teaspoon smoked paprika
- 1/4 teaspoon garlic powder
- Salt and pepper to taste

Instructions:

Preheat your grill to medium-high heat.
Brush the ears of corn lightly with olive oil or spray them with cooking spray.
Place the corn on the preheated grill and cook, turning occasionally, until the kernels are tender and slightly charred, about 10-12 minutes. Remove from the grill and let cool slightly.
Once the corn is cool enough to handle, cut the kernels off the cobs and transfer them to a large mixing bowl.
Add the black beans, diced red bell pepper, chopped red onion, and chopped cilantro to the bowl with the grilled corn kernels. Season with salt and pepper to taste.
In a small bowl, whisk together all the ingredients for the BBQ dressing until well combined.

Pour the BBQ dressing over the salad ingredients in the mixing bowl and toss until everything is evenly coated with the dressing.
Taste and adjust the seasoning, adding more salt and pepper if needed.
Serve the Grilled Corn and Black Bean Salad with BBQ Dressing immediately as a flavorful and satisfying side dish or light meal.

This Grilled Corn and Black Bean Salad with BBQ Dressing is bursting with smoky, tangy flavors and is perfect for summer cookouts, picnics, or as a healthy and refreshing meal. Enjoy!

BBQ Chickpea Wraps

Ingredients:

For the BBQ Chickpeas:

- 2 cans (15 oz each) chickpeas, drained and rinsed
- 1/2 cup barbecue sauce (ensure it's vegan)
- 1 tablespoon olive oil
- 1 teaspoon smoked paprika
- 1/2 teaspoon garlic powder
- Salt and pepper to taste

For the Wraps:

- 4 large whole wheat or spinach wraps
- 1 cup shredded lettuce or mixed greens
- 1/2 cup shredded carrots
- 1/2 cup diced tomatoes
- 1/4 cup diced red onion
- 1/4 cup chopped fresh cilantro
- Vegan ranch dressing or tahini sauce for drizzling (optional)

Instructions:

Preheat your oven to 400°F (200°C).
In a large mixing bowl, combine the drained and rinsed chickpeas with barbecue sauce, olive oil, smoked paprika, garlic powder, salt, and pepper. Stir until the chickpeas are evenly coated with the sauce.
Spread the BBQ chickpeas in a single layer on a baking sheet lined with parchment paper.
Bake in the preheated oven for 20-25 minutes, stirring halfway through, or until the chickpeas are crispy and slightly caramelized.
While the chickpeas are baking, prepare the wraps. Lay out the wraps on a flat surface.
Divide the shredded lettuce or mixed greens, shredded carrots, diced tomatoes, diced red onion, and chopped fresh cilantro evenly among the wraps, placing the ingredients in the center of each wrap.

Once the BBQ chickpeas are done baking, remove them from the oven and let them cool for a few minutes.
Spoon the BBQ chickpeas onto each wrap on top of the other ingredients.
If desired, drizzle vegan ranch dressing or tahini sauce over the BBQ chickpeas.
Roll up the wraps tightly, folding in the sides as you go.
Slice the wraps in half diagonally and serve immediately, or wrap them in parchment paper or foil for a portable meal.

These BBQ Chickpea Wraps are packed with flavor, protein, and fiber, making them a satisfying and nutritious meal option for lunch or dinner. Enjoy!

Grilled Romaine Lettuce with BBQ Drizzle

Ingredients:

- 2 heads of Romaine lettuce, halved lengthwise
- Olive oil for brushing
- Salt and pepper to taste
- BBQ sauce for drizzling
- Optional toppings: chopped tomatoes, sliced red onions, croutons, vegan cheese, etc.

Instructions:

Preheat your grill to medium-high heat.
Brush the cut sides of the Romaine lettuce halves with olive oil and sprinkle with salt and pepper.
Place the Romaine lettuce halves cut side down on the preheated grill.
Grill for 2-3 minutes, or until grill marks appear and the lettuce begins to wilt slightly.
Carefully remove the grilled Romaine lettuce halves from the grill and transfer them to a serving platter.
Drizzle BBQ sauce over the grilled Romaine lettuce halves.
Optional: Sprinkle chopped tomatoes, sliced red onions, croutons, vegan cheese, or any other desired toppings over the grilled lettuce.
Serve the Grilled Romaine Lettuce with BBQ Drizzle immediately as a unique and flavorful side dish or appetizer.

Grilling the Romaine lettuce adds a smoky flavor and a hint of char, while the BBQ drizzle adds sweetness and tanginess. Enjoy this creative and delicious twist on a salad!

BBQ Portobello Mushroom Tacos

Ingredients:

For the BBQ Portobello Mushrooms:

- 4 large portobello mushrooms, stems removed
- 1/2 cup barbecue sauce (ensure it's vegan)
- 2 tablespoons olive oil
- 1 tablespoon soy sauce or tamari
- 1 teaspoon smoked paprika
- 1/2 teaspoon garlic powder
- Salt and pepper to taste

For the Tacos:

- 8 small tortillas (corn or flour)
- BBQ Portobello Mushrooms
- 1 cup shredded lettuce or cabbage
- 1/2 cup diced tomatoes
- 1/4 cup diced red onion
- 1/4 cup chopped fresh cilantro
- Lime wedges for serving
- Optional toppings: sliced avocado, vegan cheese, jalapeños, etc.

Instructions:

Preheat your grill or grill pan to medium-high heat.
In a small bowl, whisk together the barbecue sauce, olive oil, soy sauce or tamari, smoked paprika, garlic powder, salt, and pepper to create the marinade.
Brush both sides of the portobello mushrooms with the marinade.
Place the mushrooms on the preheated grill and cook for 4-5 minutes on each side, or until tender and charred, basting with additional marinade if desired.
Remove from the grill and let cool slightly.
Once cooled, slice the portobello mushrooms into thin strips.
Warm the tortillas on the grill or in a skillet until soft and pliable.
Assemble the tacos by placing a generous portion of sliced portobello mushrooms onto each tortilla.

Top the mushrooms with shredded lettuce or cabbage, diced tomatoes, diced red onion, and chopped fresh cilantro.
Squeeze fresh lime juice over the tacos and add any optional toppings, such as sliced avocado, vegan cheese, or jalapeños.
Serve the BBQ Portobello Mushroom Tacos hot, and enjoy!

These BBQ Portobello Mushroom Tacos are savory, smoky, and packed with flavor.

They're perfect for a quick and satisfying meal that's sure to please vegans and

non-vegans alike. Customize the toppings to suit your taste preferences and enjoy!

Vegan BBQ Pasta Salad

Ingredients:

- 8 ounces (about 2 cups) pasta of your choice (such as fusilli, penne, or rotini)
- 1 cup cherry tomatoes, halved
- 1 cup cucumber, diced
- 1/2 cup red bell pepper, diced
- 1/4 cup red onion, finely chopped
- 1/4 cup black olives, sliced
- 1/4 cup fresh parsley, chopped
- 1/4 cup fresh cilantro, chopped (optional)
- Salt and pepper to taste

For the BBQ Dressing:

- 1/2 cup vegan mayonnaise
- 1/4 cup barbecue sauce (ensure it's vegan)
- 2 tablespoons apple cider vinegar
- 1 tablespoon maple syrup or agave nectar
- 1 teaspoon Dijon mustard
- 1/2 teaspoon smoked paprika
- Salt and pepper to taste

Instructions:

Cook the pasta according to the package instructions until al dente. Drain and rinse with cold water to stop the cooking process. Let it cool completely.
In a large mixing bowl, combine the cooked and cooled pasta with the halved cherry tomatoes, diced cucumber, diced red bell pepper, finely chopped red onion, sliced black olives, chopped fresh parsley, and chopped fresh cilantro (if using).
In a small bowl, whisk together all the ingredients for the BBQ dressing until well combined. Adjust the seasoning to taste with salt and pepper.
Pour the BBQ dressing over the pasta and vegetable mixture in the large mixing bowl. Toss until everything is evenly coated with the dressing.
Taste and adjust the seasoning, adding more salt and pepper if needed.
Cover the bowl with plastic wrap or a lid and refrigerate for at least 30 minutes to allow the flavors to meld together.

Before serving, give the Vegan BBQ Pasta Salad a final toss and adjust the seasoning if necessary.

Serve the Vegan BBQ Pasta Salad cold as a delicious and flavorful side dish or light meal.

This Vegan BBQ Pasta Salad is creamy, tangy, and packed with fresh vegetables, making it the perfect dish for picnics, potlucks, or any summer gathering. Enjoy!

Grilled Veggie Quesadillas with BBQ Sauce

Ingredients:

- 4 large flour tortillas
- 1 cup vegan cheese (shredded, such as cheddar or mozzarella)
- 1 cup mixed grilled vegetables (such as bell peppers, zucchini, mushrooms, onions)
- 1/4 cup barbecue sauce (ensure it's vegan)
- 2 tablespoons olive oil or cooking spray

Instructions:

Preheat a grill or grill pan over medium heat.
Place the mixed grilled vegetables on the grill and cook for 5-7 minutes, or until tender and slightly charred. Remove from the grill and set aside.
Lay out two of the flour tortillas on a flat surface.
Sprinkle vegan cheese evenly over each tortilla.
Arrange the grilled vegetables evenly over the cheese on one of the tortillas.
Drizzle barbecue sauce over the grilled vegetables.
Place the other tortilla on top to cover the vegetables and cheese, creating a quesadilla.
Brush both sides of each quesadilla with olive oil or lightly spray with cooking spray.
Place the quesadillas on the grill and cook for 3-4 minutes on each side, or until golden brown and crispy, and the cheese is melted.
Remove the quesadillas from the grill and let them cool for a minute before slicing.
Slice each quesadilla into wedges and serve hot.

These Grilled Veggie Quesadillas with BBQ Sauce are flavorful, satisfying, and perfect for a quick and delicious meal. Enjoy the combination of smoky grilled vegetables, melted cheese, and tangy barbecue sauce!

BBQ Tofu Stir Fry

Ingredients:

- 14 oz (400g) extra-firm tofu, pressed and cubed
- 2 tablespoons soy sauce or tamari
- 2 tablespoons barbecue sauce (ensure it's vegan)
- 1 tablespoon olive oil or sesame oil
- 1 onion, thinly sliced
- 2 cloves garlic, minced
- 1 bell pepper, thinly sliced
- 1 cup broccoli florets
- 1 cup sliced mushrooms
- Cooked rice or noodles for serving
- Optional toppings: sesame seeds, chopped green onions

Instructions:

In a bowl, mix together the soy sauce or tamari and barbecue sauce.
Add the cubed tofu to the sauce mixture and gently toss to coat. Let it marinate for about 15-30 minutes.
Heat olive oil or sesame oil in a large skillet or wok over medium-high heat.
Add the marinated tofu to the skillet, reserving any leftover marinade. Cook the tofu for about 5-7 minutes, or until golden brown and slightly crispy. Remove the tofu from the skillet and set aside.
In the same skillet, add sliced onion and minced garlic. Stir-fry for 2-3 minutes, until fragrant.
Add sliced bell pepper, broccoli florets, and sliced mushrooms to the skillet. Cook for another 5-7 minutes, or until the vegetables are tender-crisp.
Return the cooked tofu to the skillet and pour in the reserved marinade. Stir well to combine and cook for another 2-3 minutes, until everything is heated through.
Serve the BBQ tofu stir-fry over cooked rice or noodles.
Garnish with sesame seeds and chopped green onions, if desired.
Enjoy your delicious BBQ Tofu Stir Fry!

This flavorful stir-fry combines the smoky taste of barbecue sauce with crispy tofu and a variety of colorful vegetables for a satisfying meal. Adjust the ingredients and seasonings according to your taste preferences.

Vegan BBQ Nachos

Ingredients:

- 1 bag (about 10 oz) tortilla chips
- 1 can (15 oz) black beans, drained and rinsed
- 1 cup vegan cheese shreds (cheddar, mozzarella, or a blend)
- 1/2 cup barbecue sauce (ensure it's vegan)
- 1/2 cup diced tomatoes
- 1/4 cup diced red onion
- 1/4 cup sliced black olives
- 1 jalapeño, sliced (optional)
- 1/4 cup chopped fresh cilantro
- Guacamole, salsa, vegan sour cream, or any other desired toppings

Instructions:

Preheat your oven to 375°F (190°C).
Spread the tortilla chips evenly on a large baking sheet lined with parchment paper or aluminum foil.
Sprinkle the drained and rinsed black beans evenly over the tortilla chips.
Scatter the vegan cheese shreds over the chips and beans.
Drizzle the barbecue sauce evenly over the nachos.
Sprinkle the diced tomatoes, diced red onion, sliced black olives, and sliced jalapeño (if using) over the top of the nachos.
Place the baking sheet in the preheated oven and bake for 10-12 minutes, or until the cheese is melted and bubbly.
Remove the nachos from the oven and sprinkle the chopped fresh cilantro over the top.
Serve the Vegan BBQ Nachos hot, with guacamole, salsa, vegan sour cream, or any other desired toppings on the side.

These Vegan BBQ Nachos are perfect for sharing with friends or enjoying as a flavorful appetizer or snack. Customize the toppings to suit your taste preferences, and enjoy the delicious combination of smoky barbecue flavors and crunchy tortilla chips!

Grilled Peach Slices with BBQ Glaze

Ingredients:

- 4 ripe peaches, halved and pitted
- 1/4 cup barbecue sauce (ensure it's vegan)
- 2 tablespoons maple syrup or agave nectar
- 1 tablespoon olive oil
- 1/2 teaspoon smoked paprika
- Pinch of salt

Instructions:

Preheat your grill to medium-high heat.
In a small bowl, whisk together the barbecue sauce, maple syrup or agave nectar, olive oil, smoked paprika, and a pinch of salt until well combined.
Place the peach halves on a plate or shallow dish, cut side up.
Brush the cut side of each peach half generously with the BBQ glaze mixture.
Once the grill is hot, place the peach halves on the grill grates, cut side down.
Grill the peaches for about 3-4 minutes, or until grill marks form and they begin to soften.
Carefully flip the peaches using tongs and brush the skin side with more BBQ glaze.
Grill for an additional 2-3 minutes, or until the peaches are tender and caramelized.
Remove the grilled peach halves from the grill and transfer them to a serving platter.
Drizzle any remaining BBQ glaze over the grilled peaches.
Serve the Grilled Peach Slices with BBQ Glaze hot as a delicious dessert or side dish.

These Grilled Peach Slices with BBQ Glaze are perfect for summer cookouts or as a unique addition to your barbecue menu. Enjoy the sweet and smoky flavors of these grilled peaches!

www.ingramcontent.com/pod-product-compliance
Lightning Source LLC
LaVergne TN
LVHW081610060526
838201LV00054B/2184